# A Collection Of Shorts

Katie A Nimmo

# DEDICATION

Dedicated to my Uncle Ben, who sadly passed away before this book was completed.

# CONTENTS

# ACKNOWLEDGMENTS

In this part of this book of short stories I would like to thank all those who have inspired the characters and plots of these stories. Special thanks go out to my family who all supported me during the construction of this collection.

# 1. IVY TEAS

"Can't you just imagine it Anna? Six tables and a counter with so many different buns and teacakes you wouldn't know where to start."

Peering through the grimy shop window Anna saw a dark abandoned store that looked like it had never been loved. "Oh Elsie, I really wish I could. But all I see is cobwebs and lots of them." Elsie was crestfallen. Anna immediately regretted not siding with her friend. She had always wanted to run her own teashop but money had always left it a dream. That was until three months ago when Elsie's only aunt, Ivy, passed away leaving her enough money to get a deposit for a small store. Ivy and Elsie were going to do business together some time, but sadly that time never came.

"I'm sure Andrew will help with all the carpentry." Elsie said as she opened the door to the cobwebbed darkness. "He's ever so good at making things." She added.

"He'd do anything for you, you know that. He's loved you since forever." Anna giggled back to Elsie.

"He is a darling." Elsie smiled to herself. "I just don't think I'm good enough for Andrew."

"Andrew does what?"

Spinning round Anna and Elsie saw Andrew standing in the doorway. A tall lean man, with auburn hair and a boyish grin that looked out of place against his well groomed appearance. Despite being in a rich family Andrew loved nothing more than to get his hands on a building project, anything to have the satisfaction of creating something out of nothing.

"Thought my ears were burning," Andrew grinned as he strolled in from the doorway.

"Don't miss anything do you Andy," Anna laughed.

"No, I don't really," he laughed back. "So Elsie," he continued. "Got any plans for this place yet?"

"Well I was thinking about having a counter over here with a glass front to keep the flies away. A shelf running along the wall to hold pots of lovely flowers that will make it smell like spring every day and....." Elsie paused as she realized Andrew was gazing at her. Feeling her cheeks turn a rosy red she continued. "I also thought five or maybe six tables and perhaps, just perhaps, if I can make a success I could extend out the back to make a little garden with some more tables." Elsie looked at her feet as she finished, a little embarrassed at her long speech about her dream tea shop.

"Well, I think it sounds wonderful. I should like to be your first customer." Anna put her arm round Elsie sensing her embarrassment. "Plus my sister and I would be more than happy to help with a little gardening."

"Thank you Anna, that would be so kind." Elsie gave her hug, a big smile on her face.

"Well, I'd better get on."Andrew suddenly announced making the girls jump. "Things to do, people to see." He added as moved off toward the door of the store.

"Thanks for coming by Andrew." Anna smiled shyly. With a tip of his hat Andrew departed.

"Did I say something?" Anna enquired as Andrew disappeared out of sight.

"I don't know Elsie, I really don't know."


During the next week Elsie suffered with a nasty virus that left her under care indoors, away from her new beloved store. With spring approaching fast Elsie dipped into despair as she wanted to have her shop ready to welcome the warmer months. Feeling fed up of being bedridden, she lost hope of getting her store open in time to savor the sunshine. Regular visits from Anna didn't make her feel any better and Andrew seemed to have stopped talking to her altogether. "What did I do wrong Anna?"

"I'm going to tell you what I say every time you ask me," Anna started, "I'm sure Andrew will be in touch soon." Anna left Elsie's room with a knowing smirk on her face.

"Elsie! It's great to see you out and about again." Anna grabbed her friend in a big hug of delight.

"Anna, whatever is wrong with you? You're acting like you haven't seen me in years." Elsie shrugged off her friend's over amorous hug.

"I'm just pleased to see you." Anna grinned, in an overly cheery manner.

"Anna , I know you well enough to know when you're up to something and trying to hide it." Elsie scorned at Anna. Being friends with Anna for 7 years meant she knew her every face for every emotion, and this face was saying she was hiding something.

"What could I possibly be hiding from you?" Anna asked slyly.

"I'm not sure. That is what worries me." Elsie smiled. "But while I figure out what that is I would really like to do some work in my store since I haven't seen it in nearly five weeks."

With that Elsie and Anna strolled down the lane in to the village to endure a day's work in the store.

Getting near the end of the lane Elsie noticed a gathering of people in the street. "I wonder what's going on Anna? Look at all those people. Maybe something's happened."

"Maybe it has." Anna glanced over to her friend who had a slightly concerned look on her face.

"My store!" Elsie exclaimed. "Why are they gathering there? What's happened?" Dashing as fast as she could Elsie approached her store fearing the worst. However, on getting closer to the store she noticed something peculiar. Her once old and unloved store had a new lick of white paint on the front and was decorated with trellises strung with ivy. A sign hung over the door reading Ivy Teas. Elsie gasped as she put her hands to her mouth. A hand appeared on her shoulder, making her jump.

"What do you think Elsie?" Anna asked, beaming at her friend.

"I....I...don't know what to say." Elsie stammered. "Is this what you've been hiding from me?"

"Guilty as charged," Anna laughed. "There's more. Shall we go see?"

Lost for words Elsie was lead past the group of gathered locals reading the 'opening soon' sign pasted to the door, and taken round the back of the store. Turning the last corner the girls stopped in their tracks amazed at the sight in front of them. A quaint little garden with a cobblestone path and a fragrant smell of dozens of flowers complete with one young man stood in the centre holding a solitary rose, gazing across at them rather sheepishly.

"Andrew," Elsie whimpered. Holding back her tears of surprise and happiness. With a nudge Anna urged Elsie forward. Without saying a word Elsie slowly moved her arms round Andrew and held him in a gentle hug. "What do you think, will it do?" Andrew asked as he gave her the rose.

Looking up at the enquiring face Elsie took his hands in hers. " Only if you stay here with me. My dream store would not be complete without you."

"Elsie there is nowhere I'd rather be and you know it." They both laughed as hand in hand they went to investigate the new talk of the village Ivy Teas.

## 2. EVERGREEN COPSE PART 1

Rachel pulled her coat collar tighter round her neck as she drove herself forwards through the strong winds. The chill was biting at her face trying to push her back with an almighty force. She hated walking through the woods but it was the quickest way home. Making it worse was the fact there was no clear cut pathway leading through so one could easily lose their way and end up in the middle of nowhere off the beaten track. So many tales haunted the woods. Tales of disappearances and horrors that Rachel did not want to think about whilst in the thick of the isolated copse.

The tiny torch in her phone was not nearly enough to light a safe path through all the uplifted tree roots and hidden potholes ready to twist or even break an ankle. A sudden gust of wind made Rachel gasp as it attempted to sweep her off her feet catching her off guard, toppling sideways she fell into a tree catching her arm with a painful scrape. Letting go off her coat she grabbed hold of her arm in pain. Flying open, her coat made her look as though she had a witch's cape, ready to take flight in the high flying winds. Shuddering in the newfound cold without protection of her coat Rachel struggled to hold her mini torch with her injured arm as she ploughed through desperately trying to avoid any and all obstacles. Somewhere behind her a twig snapped. Rachel stopped dead. Her lip quivered as fear engulfed her, tales of horror suddenly springing in to her mind. Slowly turning her head she looked for where the sound came from but she could see nothing, too many trees and too much wind blowing in her eyes. Completely immobilized Rachel tried to take deep breaths to get life back into her body. Managing to bring her head back round she looked on in the direction of home giving herself a pep talk. 'Come on Rachel, you can do this. There's nothing here in the woods, it's all in your imagination. You need to get home to sort your arm out and find Nora. Must speak to Nora.' Using all her strength Rachel began to get motion back in her legs putting one in front of the other, faster and faster until she was running. A dim light appeared in the distance, civilization. With new found hope Rachel found herself rejoicing as she gained more momentum to get home as fast as she could. A hand appeared on her shoulder pulling her back, twisting round to see her attacker Rachel screamed as a blue rope enclosed around her neck.

"Good morning Nora. These are the papers for today, they all need responding to and then put on file."

"Yes of course Mr Flake." Starting on her pile of papers the everyday monotonous job of sorting through papers began yet again. Three years down the line and Nora was still stuck in the dead end job, no experience to apply for another field of work but it at least paid her bills. Settling down at the dark mahogany desk she began to sort the tower of papers that now cluttered the work top. Working as a secretary in a solicitor's bureau was interesting work but eerily quiet. Business was poor at the moment but there were a few cases still open that needed attending to. Mr Flake had set up the business many years ago as a private practice for those who could not travel to the city to have expert advice or help. Initially the bureau had been well received however a close knit community in the village meant not a lot happened really. Everyone got along with everyone and there were no issues that needed soliciting. The first file of the day was a settlement of planning permission. The Roserants wanted to build a conservatory on to the rear of their house, today is the day they get permission to do so. Next on the agenda same photocopying needed doing in the stationers next door, being on the high street certainly came in handy sometimes. Shrugging on her fur collared coat Nora started down the staircase down to the reception.

"Nora?" A voice called from the top of the stairs.

"Yes Mr Flake?" She answered from halfway down the stairs.

"Have you seen Miss Lempsey this morning? She is running late with my morning tea. Give her a nudge will you please."

With that he disappeared back in to his office and closed the door. With a sarcastic face and half curtsey Nora continued down the stairs. She had never really liked Mr Flake. 'Pompous old man.' She thought to herself. He was aging now, all alone but with piles of money. He always put himself first and definitely knew how to stand up for himself. The poor paper boy from next door knew that better than anyone, only the other morning the boy had an earful because he was running 10 minutes behind with his paper round.

Turning round the corner into the reception area Nora wondered over to the desk.

"Morning Hettie."

"Good morning Nora, you off out?"

" There and beyond to next door." Nora giggled in response. Hettie giggled with her. Hettie was a nice girl, still new to the business but learning fast. Her brown hair and bright blue eyes could turn a few heads but she was completely oblivious to the attention. The girls hushed themselves quickly in case Mr Flake heard them, he ran a very tight ship and despised any sound or sight of happiness in his building.

"His Lordship wants to know where Rachel has got to with his morning tea, goodness forbid it hasn't arrived yet." Nora grinned at Hettie as she nodded in agreement.

"I can't say I've seen her this morning. She might have had to get more milk or something from down the street." Hettie replied as she shrugged her skinny shoulders.

"Maybe. Anyway see you in a minute." With a little tap on the reception desk Nora moved off to continue her venture to the stationers. It was only a tiny store that sold a few pens, envelopes and local papers but it was charming. An old building that had beams running across the ceiling and windows that let in too much breeze, wearing a jacket indoors was essential. Walking in the boy at the counter knew straight away what Nora was there for so promptly asked how many and what size. Prepping her order the boy moved quickly as was aware that any delay would result in another ear bashing from Mr Flake. Nora took advantage of the five minute break to flick through a couple of newspapers. Nothing exciting in there today, lots of advertisements for the car boot sale and a couple of buildings crumbling, apart from that nothing to get worked up about. Retrieving her order of papers Nora paid and made her way back into the seemingly colder solicitor's bureau.

"George working as fast as always I see." Hettie laughed as Nora walked back in, hinting at how fast she'd been there and back.

"Yes," she laughed. "He really doesn't like him does he." Dropping the receipt on the desk Nora gave her daily account of what was in the newspapers and what was not going on in the village. After discovering that once again there was no gossip to learn of Hettie suggested getting back before a certain someone thought they were taking too long doing something. With a sigh Nora retired back to her duties and climbed up the stairs whilst leaving Hettie to her telephone that wasn't ringing.

Plumping herself back at her own desk at the top of the stairs Nora filtered through the newly photocopied papers, organizing them into separate piles ready to be stapled or filed. Reaching down to collect staples from the bottom drawer Nora sat back up with a little jump, startled that out of nowhere Mr Flake was stood right in front of her desk glaring at her.

"Are your ears quite functioning Miss Robin?" He remarked still glaring at her.

"Why yes sir." Nora replied quite astounded by the abrupt insinuation. Running through her mind she couldn't think if she'd missed anything, had she forgotten something.

"I'm very sure that I told you that my tea had not arrived twenty five minutes ago and do you know, it still isn't here." Leaning forward onto the counter his piercing eyes looked right into Nora's. Nora found herself unwillingly leaning back in her chair as he leaned forward. "I really do not think that is a difficult task to sort out, do you? You'll do it now." Pushing himself off her desk he strode back into his office and slammed the door. Nora was left speechless. After her temporary paralysation she got up and when back down to the reception.

"What on earth was that all about?" Hettie called as she saw a pale faced Nora come back down the stairs.

"His precious morning tea still hasn't arrived." Nora replied in a half stroppy manner. "Sorry Hettie, I don't mean to be off with you. He really gets me sometimes. Where is Rachel though?"

"That's alright, I know. He does it to me too occasionally. I don't know where she is, I still haven't seen her." Hettie now wore a slightly worried look on her face, trying to think of when she last saw her. "I'm sure she said she was going last night for a drink with someone straight after here but she would have gone home. Unless she isn't well?" Hettie suggested.

"Perhaps. Maybe we should call her home to check if she's ok." Nora said. "Whilst I sort out the tea." Nora added rolling her eyes. Drifting off to the kitchen the tea was made and taken up to the office while Hettie telephoned Rachel's home to enquire after her. With a sarcastic and impertinent manner Nora was dismissed from the office with comment muttered behind her as she closed the door. Taking a deep breath she once again climbed down the stairs to replace the tea tray. "Any news Hettie?" Nora asked propping herself on the reception desk.

"Well yes and no really." Hettie answered looking confused. "Yes I managed to speak to her sister at home but apparently she never came home last night. They have police out looking for her."

All colour dropped from Nora's face. "Well what's happened to her?" Her lip started to tremble.

"I don't know Nora. I really don't know."

# 3. THYME'S A WINNER

"Rosie! Good morning!" Snapping out of her daydream Rosie lowered her newspaper to see her neighbor looking at her over the garden fence.

"Good morning Alfred! You gave me quite a fright." She laughed, laying her paper down on the table.

"Oh, I'm sorry. I can be a bit loud I guess." Alfred laughed back. Peering over the fence was what Alfred did best. A nosy character but harmless all the same. "I see you're already reading today's paper. Was going to ask if you'd seen the local news bit yet but you're almost done there so I expect you have."

"I skimmed through it yes, but I don't really read it properly, village gossip travels quite well by itself without the aid of a newspaper." Rosie said matter of factly, Alfred was nodding in agreement.

"You're not wrong Rosie. Only yesterday did old Bertie say his pocket watch was missing and in not ten minutes half the village was looking for it. Meaning either this village is full of gossipers or those who have too much time on their hands, or even worse...both!" Laughing even harder this time Alfred wiped the tears from his eyes. "Anyway," he continued trying to compose himself. "I actually wondered if you'd read about the fair this year. How they're having a new contest this year."

"The herb contest you mean? Yes I did see that. It'll be nice to have a little extension to our fair. But you know I don't care much for competitions." Getting off her chair Rosie handed Alfred a handkerchief to help dry the tears off his face.

"Thanks Rosie. Yes I know you don't like competition. Would be fun though wouldn't it, don't you think? Bit of friendly fun to bring the best herbs from your lovely collection there." He gestured towards Rosie's herb garden half way up the garden surrounded by brickwork and cobbles. The herb garden was Rosie's pride and joy, with basil and thyme and a hint of rosemary, a walk in the garden was a pleasure with such a fresh scent.

"You know most of the village is talking about it. All of a sudden these little herb gardens are popping up all over the place which have supposedly been in their gardens for years. I'll wash this for you." Waving the handkerchief Alfred put it in his waistcoat pocket.

"That doesn't surprise me Alfred." Rosie giggled. Several people practically bounced to mind who would try to pull that trick off. Alfred was speaking the truth though, nobody cared for their herbs like Rosie did. Every other garden in the village was full of English roses and other flowers to make them look appealing, no sign of herbs anywhere.

"At least have a think about it Rosie. Might be fun." With a little flurry Alfred disappeared from the fence, leaving Rosie alone with her thoughts. Even as a child she had never liked competition, she'd never won anything in her life so she stopped trying and started living her own life, enjoying what she loved.

"Rosie!"

"Alfred! I wish you would stop doing that.." Huffing at him for making her jump twice in the space of one morning.

"Sorry. Again. Just remembered. You do know that Deidre is entering?" Alfred raised an eyebrow, waiting for a reaction.

"Deidre?" Rosie pondered for a moment. "Deidre doesn't know the first thing about herbs, why is she entering?" Her voice getting to hysterical tones.

"One plain reason. Without you in the competition she knows she's as good as won already." Shrugging his shoulders he started to move away again.

"But Deidre wins everything, surely she'd give someone else a chance?"

"You think? No one else enters when she's competing. saves the heartache of knowing you're going to lose. Unless another participant makes a stand this year at the new herb contest." Gazing at Rosie, Alfred said nothing more and disappeared for good this time with a smirk on his face.

Saturday, the day of the fair, soon arrived to be welcomed by glorious sunshine. A perfect day for a village fair. 6 am saw the first of the tents being set upon the village green. The tea tent was always the most popular, with a selection of teas and freshly made cakes and scones it was easy to see why it was popular. One by one other tents erected on the green with an array of items and activities. A raffle with toys and a stall selling homemade greetings cards, there was a bit of everything.

10 am arrived and the whole village came out to enjoy the annual fair. The children had hours of fun going on the carousel and playing games with the entertainers whilst the adults lapped up the treat of cream teas in the ever popular tea tent.

The afternoon was traditionally used for all contests during the annual fair.

Judges would walk around the village looking at all the gardens with their beautiful roses. Then returning to try any entrants for the pickles and preserves contest.

"Rosie, you made it!" Alfred hobbled over as she entered the main tent.

"Hello Alfred. Yes can't be the only one sat at home can I? Thought I'd join the crowd for a change." Despite the festivities happening around them, Rosie appeared to be a minor celebrity as it was well known she didn't come out to the fair. At least twenty people came to say hello and thanks for coming, Rosie felt quite loved. A feeling she didn't expect from attending a fair she hadn't been to for many years.

"Rosie, I do believe you're just as popular as the tea tent." Alfred laughed nudging her with his elbow. Holding on to his elbow Rosie began to laugh as well until someone ploughed into the back of her. Spinning round she wasn't surprised at who it was. Glaring at her down her nose was Deidre.

"You should really watch where you stand Rosie dear, you'll get knocked over." Looking her up and down Deidre moved off further into the tent.

"What a piece of work." Alfred remarked. "Really thinks she's all that." Shaking his head with disgust he went on his rounds to gossip with the ladies from the post office.

Watching after Deidre, Rosie stood alone like she had for most of her life. Always being made to feel inferior and unimportant. Deidre's walk annoyed her, strolling around like she owned the place all because she had the biggest house in the village, and the money to go with it. Not to mention the fact that she frightens away any friendly competition at the fairs to make sure she won. 'Well,' Rosie thought to herself. 'This year is going to be different.' As if on cue an announcement went out on the loudspeakers saying the herb contest was about to begin. All attention was diverted towards the mini stage in the tent.

"Ladies and gentleman here we all are for our first ever herb contest." A big round of applause rang round the tent as the local vicar introduced the event. "As you all know we have held our best garden and best rose contests for some years now with the addition of our preserves and pickles contest last year." Another ripple of applause, with most people glancing over at Deidre who seemed to be making her way to the front already. "So this year it gives me a privilege to welcome a new contest to our little fair to see which garden can grow the best tasting and smelling herbs. The judging has been carried out during the course of the afternoon and the votes were unanimous." Before the vicar had even finished Deidre was already on the stage and practically had her hands on the little trophy for first prize.

Moving the trophy away from her grappling hands, the tent fell silent as the vicar continued. "The winning entry for this year's herb contest was a late entry submitted only this morning." Whispers went round the room as Deidre's face fell. There had never been anyone to compete against her in anything. "Our winner for the best thyme in the village goes to Rosie!" Gasps filled the room, quickly followed by a huge round of applause which was deafening. Rosie walked very slowly up on to the stage with Deidre scowling at her from the side, cheers went through the tent. Taking the little trophy from the vicar Rosie gave a curt little wave into the crowd of people who were beaming at her. "Rosie congratulations. Thank you so much for entering, you've been an inspiration to all these people." The vicar said quietly as he shook Rosie's hands. "Now, Rosie," he said over the loudspeaker. "Is there anything you'd like to say?"

Raising her trophy in the air, tears of joy ran down her face and she quietly said "thyme's a winner." Alfred and a dozen other villagers swarmed Rosie hugging her and congratulating her as Deidre skulked out of the tent forgotten.

# 4. TINSEL TREE

"I think it looks better round my neck, like a scarf!" Angela giggled as she strutted around the sitting room as if on a catwalk, even posing in front of the mirror on the wall.

"Get out of the way! You messed up my foxtrot." William complained as he stalked over to the far side of the room ready to start dancing across the floor again.

"Come on now you two. Help me finish decorating the tree so we can switch the lights on." Mum scorned. Christmas really could be hard work sometimes.

"OK mummy." Angela replied. Whipping the tinsel off from around her neck ,she hung it around the fish tank, in the corner of the room then sidled over to the tree. Kneeling on the floor she grabbed hold of the nearest bag of decorations and started rummaging.

"Come on William, you too."Mum added.

"But I don't like the white lights, I like the coloured ones." William complained sulkily.

"How about if we put both sets of lights on the tree so you can have the coloured lights and me and daddy can have the white ones?" Mum suggested.

"OK." William huffed as he joined Angela at the base of the tree. "I want to put them on though." He added.

"Alright William just do it slowly so we don't get them tangled up. Here we go I'll hold the lights and you can lay them on the tree." Mum took hold of the bundle of lights as a safety measure. Untangling the lights after a year in the loft was a nightmare already without the added tangles of an 8 year old boy putting them on a tree in a half hazard way.

"Mummy? Can I put some of the tartan presents on the tree?" Angela asked, with two mini present shaped baubles on her fingers.

"Just a minute Angela, let William finish putting the lights on the tree then you can put them wherever you like." Angela was nine and was always keen to get stuck in with her hands and decorate things. She even liked knitting, which is very odd for a nine year old.

Mum and William finished putting the lights on the tree so they tucked in to the bags of decorations with Angela in the middle of them. With a nod of approval from Mum she immediately started hanging the mini presents on the tree. Angela liked the presents best out of all the decorations because Mum had made them out of sweet boxes then wrapped them in leftover tartan material from one of Angela's dresses. Which also happened to be Angela's favorite dress.

"Mummy where's your Santa?" Angela asked still burrowing through the decorations.

"He's right here on the coffee table." Reaching over to the coffee table Mum picked up a fragile paper Santa with cotton wool as a beard. "Now this Santa sits in the middle of the tree. I made him when I was a little girl." Mum told them as she sat him gently in the tree. "Are we all finished now?"

"Yes I think so mummy." Angela answered sitting back on her haunches looking up at the tree.

"Do we have to have that Santa on the tree? I don't like it." William puffed.

"Yes William he does. He's always been on mummy's tree." Mum replied roughing up his hair. Flinching away William went through to the kitchen in the hunt for food.

"I like him mummy." A little voice said from the base of the tree.

"I do too Angela. Tell you what, shall we switch the lights on?"

"Yay! Can we have the coloured ones on?" Angela asked getting up to put the plug in.

"Of course you can. Let's count them down, first time on this year, ready?" Angela's hand pausing on the plug, Mum joined her as they counted down. "3....2....1! Wooo!!" They exclaimed together.

"Pretties!" Angela said in glee, her eyes twinkling at the tree lights.

Through the wall they heard the front door open and close and a voice call out. "Hello? Anyone home?"

"Daddy!" Angela squealed as she ran from the sitting room through the kitchen and round to the front door. Throwing her arms round him she gave him a big cuddle.

"Hello you!" He kissed her head as she let go to let him walk into the kitchen. "Hello William." Not much of an answer came out of him as he had resumed his dancing round the kitchen instead. "Hello darling," he gave Mum a kiss.

"How was work today?" Mum asked filling up the kettle.

"Alright I suppose, still I'm home now and it's Christmas Eve!" Dad cheered giving Mum a hug.

"Ooh ooh daddy!! Come see the tree!!" Angela yelped as she ran from the kitchen into the sitting room. "Daddy! Come look!" She called from the other room.

Taking his coat off and hanging it on a chair in the kitchen Dad followed Angela into the sitting room and went over to the tree. "Wow look at this! But hang on the coloured lights are on, where's my white ones?" He asked Angela teasingly.

"The coloured ones are better daddy." Angela replied with a grin on her little face.

"Of course they are you're absolutely right." Putting his arm round her they walked back into the kitchen to nearly be knocked over by William's boisterous dancing.

"Come on William not in the kitchen please." Mum was saying, trying to prepare some dinner around him.

"What film are we going to watch mummy?"Angela asked appearing at Mum's elbow at the work surface, watching everything she was doing.

"Well we're going to watch a Christmas film as it's Christmas Eve, but we haven't decided on one yet." Mum remarked while wiping Angela's nose with a bit of flour, making her giggle.

"Can we play our game?" She asked.

"Which game sweetheart?" Mum replied as she walked over to the oven to put the dinner in.

"The one where we sit at the tree and try to guess what the presents are without touching them." Angela gave a cheesy grin as if to enforce the point of how exciting the game was.

"In a minute ok?"

Clapping her hands with a little jump Angela rushed into the sitting room and skidded over to kneel by the tree.

"Right we've got fifteen minutes till dinner comes out of the oven." Mum said as she sat on the sofa next to the tree.

"What do you think this one is mummy?" Angela pointed at a red parcel at the front of the tree. "I think it's a pair of slippers. I know what that one is, because I put it there. The green one there looks a bit like a book but it might not be." Mum listened to Angela pointing out all the different parcels under the tree, nodding and agreeing when she paused for breath. Dad came and sat next to Mum putting his arm round her. William came prancing in the door, still colliding with unmoving objects with his energetic dancing.

The kitchen timer rang and Mum went to retrieve the dinner out of the oven. Christmas Eve was always buffet night. With sausage rolls and crisps and a selection of pastries fresh from the oven. "Dinner," Mum called as the hungry family poured out of the sitting room. Each grabbing a plate they all piled up their nibbles and congregated in the sitting room ready to watch a Christmas film. The film started and the children were glued straight away, sitting quietly eating their feasts.

Finishing the festive feast bedtime was announced as Santa would have started his journey already. "Everyone in, quickly! He knows if you're not in bed." Mum ushered the children to their rooms at the top of the stairs. She tucked in William first who was already half asleep, warn out from his dancing antics. Angela had already got herself into bed and was nestling in when Mum arrived. Giving her a kiss Mum closed the door and disappeared into her own room.

Christmas morning soon arrived to the early alarm clock, primarily known as Angela. "He's been he's been!" She screeched as she dragged her stocking across the landing and clumsily down the stairs. William had already brought his stocking down and was watching the big turkey in the oven.

"Mum why is there foil on it?" William asked still watching the oven.

"Helps it cook darling." Mum answered. Putting breakfast on the kitchen table, consisting of hot tea and gammon sandwiches.

Coming down the stairs there was the sound of footsteps and a cheery tune of Jingle Bells. In the kitchen door Dad walked in holding his musical tie dancing and singing along in his suit and slippers. "It's Christmas!" He hollered, dancing over to the table. The children giggled as he chased Mum around the kitchen before settling for his cup of tea.

After breakfast everyone huddled into the sitting room to open a couple of stocking presents before going to church. "Remember everyone, as soon as church finishes we're coming back straight away because the turkey's in the oven."

"Yes Mum," they all replied in unison. Piling out of the front door and into the car it was time to go to church. On arrival they went into the church hall to retrieve any Christmas cards they had been left. The church had its own little postbox and cards were sorted into family piles in alphabetical order. Mum took the pile off the table and exchanged pleasantries with some family friends while Dad kept the excitable children under control.

The church service was short but full of carols and good cheer. Angela and William took part in a mini show and tell and the front to show everyone what Santa had brought them. Lots of claps and laughs went round as all the children showed their new toys even some adults joined in.

About 1 o clock Christmas dinner was served. The kitchen was full of vegetables and sauces, the smell was delightful. Crackers were pulled at the table and everyone wore their paper hats, though Angela's was too big and kept sliding down over her eyes. The mountain of washing up was conquered and all the pans cleared away. Present time was in the afternoon. One gift at a time was opened while the rest of the family watched to see delight on the others' faces.

In the evening all unwanted paper had gone to the recycling, and the children sat on the floor playing with their gifts. Mum and Dad sat down on the sofa to watch the joy as Angela and William played together.

"This is what it's all about," Dad whispered to Mum. "Family all being together. No fighting, just enjoying each other's company." Holding her hand they both watched their magical Christmas unfold as Santa looked on from his place in the middle of the tinsel tree.

# 5. LOVE FROM THE FIRE

When a policeman comes to your front door it always sets you on edge, makes you involuntarily think the worst straight away. In my case it was. Sam being a fireman always worried me, never knowing if he'd come home. Being an orphan from the age of seven I had a fear of being alone, I knew Sam could look after himself but there was always an uneasy feeling when he was called out on a job. With only my wedding ring for family I held on to it tight. The constable removed his hat as I closed my eyes and my heart sank, knowing what was coming. He sat me down and broke the news gently, telling me how it happened. Turns out Sam died a hero, saving an elderly couple from their blazing inferno of a home. My eyes welled as I thought of how much I loved him and how I'd never get to say goodbye. A hero, my hero.

"My dear, I don't know what I can say to make you feel better. Sam's in a comfortable place now covered in flowers I know he'd love."

"Thank you Mrs Price. The sun is shining so brightly today, Sam always said when he's happy the sun is happy." Remembering his smile brought a tear down my cheek. Mrs Price had been so kind. The day after I heard that awful news Mr and Mrs Price came to visit me, they were the last people to see him alive as he brought them out of their burning home.

"It's hard to believe it's been two months already." Mrs Price said delicately, as she handed me a cup of tea.

"Thank you," I said as I relished the first sip of hot sweet tea. "I know, it's been two months but it feels a lifetime."

"It'll get easier with time. I know it's hard to hear but it will. Sam won't want you to grieve for the rest of your life." Mrs Price said as she held my free hand. "I'll tell you something else too," she added. "You really don't have to call me Mrs Price, I'm Betty to my friends."

"Oh Betty," I paused and smiled at her. "I know, you're right. It's just been so hard being on my own at home and with me being under the weather these last few weeks, it's really been getting on top of me." Giving her hand a squeeze I let go to have another sip of tea.

"I'm sorry to hear you're not well deary. Nothing serious I hope." Betty's face was etched with concern.

"No not at all, just being 'ill' every morning and being a little light headed in the afternoons, I'm sure it will pass."

Betty looked at me enquiringly, put down her tea on the table and leant towards me. "Are you pregnant deary?" She whispered so Robert, Mr Price, couldn't hear from the next room.

My mouth dropped, it felt like my heart had stopped. Pregnant. Could I be? "I...I...I don't know. I don't see how, there's been no one..." I stammered. "Do you think I could be?" I added raising my hand to my face.

"It certainly sounds like it my dear, you have all the symptoms. Tell you what, tomorrow let's get you tested and find out. I'll let Robert know we're borrowing the car tomorrow." With a smile and a reassuring hug Betty disappeared.

A week later it was confirmed. Four months in, five to go. The thought of being a mummy was scary but at the same time I was excited. I had so much to think about and do, as well as create a nursery and make my home safe for an infant. Having Betty and Robert around me was so comforting, they helped me every step of the way and they even moved in to my spare room so I wasn't alone. Robert was a whiz at DIY as he handmade a cot, a bookshelf and a small chair and table. We made a great team all of us. Robert the carpenter, Betty the painter and me the waddling tea maker. As time went on we became very close and I decided that I wanted these lovely people to stay in mine and the baby's life after the birth and beyond. "My dear, nothing would give us greater pleasure," Betty sobbed. "Sorry, excuse me." I watched and smiled after Betty as she hurriedly left the room as fresh tears threatened to explode.

"Ellie," I turned to see Robert close behind me. "While Betty isn't here," he whispered, "I want to say thank you. When we were married I was told that I could not reproduce. Until this day Betty has never once held it against me. She always wanted a family. But despite my inability to give her what she always wanted, she stayed." Robert paused to wipe the tears from his eyes. Guiding me over to the corner of the room we sat on the sofa. Taking a deep breath he continued. " Betty gave up all her dreams of a family because she loved me. Never did we once think a chance of being a family would come along in our lifetime. I would like it very much if you would give us the honor of adopting you as our daughter."

Now it was my turn to well up. No words could surface. I just sat there and cried. Throwing my arms round him he held me for what seemed an eternity.

"I feel so tired Betty, but having a lovely little lady in my life makes it seem so unimportant." I looked down to my arms where my precious baby girl laid quite still, just as tired as me I imagined.

"She's beautiful Ellie." Betty whispered, her face glowing with pride.

"Betty I do believe that's the first time you've called me by my name," I giggled quietly, trying not to wake the sleeping beauty in my arms.

"Well 'deary' doesn't seem appropriate now does it. " She chuckled as she put her arm round me.

"No I suppose not," I replied smiling just as much as she was.

"Anyway, in front of this little lady my name is not Betty," she paused as I looked up at her. "It's Nanny to my family." She laughed.


Three days later the four of us took a stroll to fulfill a very important appointment. As we approached our destination my emotions got the best of me making me stop in my tracks. Robert put his hand on my shoulder. "Come on Ellie, can't keep him waiting." Smiling at him I carried on down the path. Sitting gently on the grass I affectionately stroked Sam's headstone. "Well Mr," I said to the stone. " I have someone for you to meet. Now you remember Betty and Robert," glancing over I saw them smiling down at us with their arms round each other. "And this is your daughter. Samantha." As the tears rolled down my face the sun came out from behind the clouds and smiled on us all. "I love you Sam." I whispered to the sky. Although Sam was no longer here he had given me the greatest gift in the world, a family. Mummy, baby Samantha, her newly adopted grandparents and daddy's love in all our hearts.

# 6. EVERGREEN COPSE PART 2

"I better report it to mister bigwig upstairs I suppose." Nora whispered, finding it hard to find words after learning of Rachel's disappearance.

"Best had. Can't have him being nasty about her when she isn't here to defend herself. I wouldn't put it past him though." Hettie added, also in a hushed voice.

"Right, here we go, wish me luck." Nora pulled herself off of the reception desk and gently made her way up the stairs, a little light headed after such bad news. Trying not to think the worst was very hard but hope was a little thin after a whole night of being unaccounted for. Reaching the office door she knocked on the door softly.

"Come in." A grumpy voice came from the other side of the door. On seeing there was no tea making an entrance the voice got more angry. "Still no tea? This is preposterous. I cannot see how difficult it is to make a cup of tea, I really can't. Just proves that all young girls are just as the rumors say. Young, thick and stupid."

"Mr Flake, sir." Nora started, fighting to hold back the tears.

"Oh it speaks. Well let's find out what the excuse is today shall we?" Mr Flake folded his arms and stared at her from his red cushioned chair.

"It's Rachel, sir." She said quietly. "She's been reported missing, the police are looking for her." A single tear ran down her left cheek as she said it.

"Oh right. So we're going on adventures during work time are we? Well when she reappears you can tell her she is now on the unemployment list. She is not to come back to this office, is that understood? I give her a job in my establishment and this is how she repays me?" Huffing into the air Mr Flake returned the pages on his desk. "That is all."

With that Nora knew she was being asked to leave from the office. She couldn't believe what she had just heard. A young girl, an employee, has been reported missing and all he cared about was his missing cup of tea. Shaking her head more tears fell as she closed the heavy office door carefully. If she didn't need the money so much she would leave and find another job. However there were no other sufficient vacancies in the village to apply for, not with her lack of experience in other fields. Perching on the edge Nora needed a minute to think. Wiping her tears off her face with her hands she desperately tried to think what could have happened to Rachel. They had worked together for two years and been best friends for the majority of that time. Knowing Rachel, she would have headed straight home after her drink out with her friend, whom Nora suspected a little more than a 'friend' in reality. Even if she'd been delayed she would have called her sister to let her know so she wouldn't wait up to lock up the house when she got in.

"What did he say?" A hushed voice whimpered over the edge of banister making Nora jump.

"Oh Hettie," she replied creeping over to the rail. "He doesn't care, just banging on about how she's done it deliberately and he's giving her the heave ho." The tears started again as Hettie held her hand.

"We both know he's a nasty piece of work. He only cares about himself, no wonder he doesn't have a wife or family." She was right, Nora thought to herself. Mr Flake had been a bachelor all his life so he says. A miserable old man with no cares for anyone or anything except his money and precious cups of morning tea. In fact no one in the village liked or invited him anywhere unless they were newcomers and didn't know any different. "How about we pop round her house later to see Hazel. I'm sure she'd appreciate some company." Hazel, Rachel's older sister was very fond of her sibling and devoted to looking after her since their parents died many years ago.

They really were two peas in a pod, inseparable and so important to each other.

"Yes, I think that would be a good idea." Nora sniffed trying to stop the next onslaught of tears. Hearing movement in the office they both darted their separate ways, Nora to her desk and Hettie down the stairs, just in time for Mr Flake to appear at the office door.

"Make an appointment at 3.30 for Mr Michaels to come in and sign his papers. Now." Just us abruptly Mr Flake disappeared back into his office. With a sigh Nora did as she was asked and continued to work as much as she could to keep her mind occupied for the rest of the afternoon.

5.30 came and both girls kept the date and walked over to Rachel's home to see her sister Hazel. Opening the door she looked a state, her face pale and soaked with tears her hair a mess where she hadn't tamed it and big black circles under eyes from lack of sleep.

"Oh Hazel." Hettie said as she threw her arms round her as Hazel cried into her shoulder. Walking her indoors the girls put the kettle on and wrapped Hazel up in blankets making sure she was comfortable. Her front room was a mess. Used tissues all over the floor, sofa cushions by the window where she'd been sat waiting for Rachel to come home and cold cups of tea sitting everyplace imaginable.

"Still no news?" Nora asked sitting down at the dining table. Shaking her head Hazel found no words to reply with. Nora exchanged a glance with Hettie who was holding hazel's hand, both frantically thinking of something to say to make it better. Sitting in silence the knock on the door made everyone jump. Nora jumped up to answer the door to find it was Albert from the greengrocers.

"Hello Albert." Nora said attempting to make half a smile.

"Hi Nora sweetheart. Hazel here?" He spoke in a husky voice that sounded strained.

"Yes she's in the sitting room, come in." Stepping aside Nora let Alfred in. He wiped his feet on the mat as he held his hat tightly in his hands. Walking into the sitting room the other girls looked up at him from the sofa.

"I came straight here." Alfred started, his knuckles getting whiter as he held onto his hat tighter. "Thought it would be better coming from me. I'm so sorry." Alfred started to sob, looking down at his hat. "So sorry." He stuttered trying to get his words out. "They've found her." An eerie silence took hold of the room as all the girls realized what Alfred was trying to tell them. A new hold of grief took over as Hazel wept uncontrollably, Hettie held on to her as much as she could. Taking Alfred's arm Nora moved him over to the window.

"Where is she?" She whispered, out of earshot from the others in the room.

"In the woods. On the floor. Right near your house. She's been strangled." Alfred spoke partially through his sobs. Nora gasped her hands flying to her mouth, new tears welling up.

"Maybe she was coming to visit me then, last night. Probably coming to tell me about her date. But why didn't she call me?" Nora stroked her hand through her hair, contemplating different reasons as to why Rachel had been behaving out of character.

Hazel stood up behind them and slowly tiptoed towards them at the window. "Can I see her?" She asked simply. Looking at Alfred he nodded. All the girls put the coats and shoes on and Alfred took them round to Nora's house then into the woods opposite. Before they got there they could see where she was. A group of policemen and a cordon were visible close to the exit of the woods amongst the trees and bracken. As they got closer a policeman came over to them.

"Sorry all of you, no spectators." He made to move them away but Alfred explained that Hazel was the dead girl's sister and only living family member. After quiet deliberation Alfred managed to persuade the policeman to take Hazel to see her. Watching from a distance the little group saw Hazel completely break down, confirming the news, it was

Rachel.

Running down the lane a young man dressed in blue overalls and brown jacket approached the group. "Ben?" Nora exclaimed as he arrived. Out of breath he hugged Nora and the girls then shook Alfred's hand.

"It's true isn't it?" He puffed glancing over at the crime scene in front of them. "As soon as I heard I came straight over to yours."

"How come you didn't go over to Rachel's.....I mean Hazel's house?" Nora asked really confused over the blatant lack of order of importance. Surely the family come first not the friends in such a situation as this.

"Well you would have been the last person to see her alive?" He remarked, as if it was obvious.

"Me? But How? I didn't see her after work, she left to go out for a drink with someone after work that was the last I saw her, I swear." Nora was speaking hysterically, realizing that she could be a prime suspect in her best friend's death.

"Well she was out with me, wasn't she." Ben said, suddenly throwing light on how he knew where to come when he heard the news. "When we were out she had a bit of an episode in the pub. Looked like she'd seen a ghost then suddenly announced she needed to see you. Sounded urgent. She was coming to yours straight after."

"But Ben she never got to mine last night. What did she want to tell me?" Nora asked taking his hands tightly.

"I don't know. She wouldn't tell me." Ben stammered under the pressure of Nora's gaze. "Now she'll never tell anyone." The group fell silent as they all watched over the scene in the woods. Hazel kneeling over her dead sibling surrounded by policemen.

"Whatever it was," Alfred muttered. "She died for it." Looking away from the scene, Hazel was left holding her sister unknowing of the reason her one sibling had been taken from her.

# 7. AURA

Sergeant Grey ran as fast as he could down the dark cobbled street after his mark. fifteen minutes of solid running was starting to take its toll. How they could keep it up was an absolute wonder, how can they not be tiring yet? So many corners and jumping walls, the athleticism of some people is astonishing. Jumping down from yet another wall, seemingly higher this time, Grey found himself in a graveyard. Crossing his chest he quietly apologized in case he ran across someone's grave during his pursuit. Scrunching up his nose there was an awful smell, bit like weed Grey made note.

Movement to the left, off his feet quicker than a cat he ran across the yard towards the movement in the distance. Fog was setting in making it difficult to see his subject and the obstacles in the graveyard. Stopping short Grey made it to the wall bordering the church. Fifteen feet high. No way they could have jumped that Grey thought to himself scanning his surroundings. Grabbing his radio from his chest he reported in.

"Grey to control. Subject escaped. Lost in Aura graveyard headed east. Returning to post. Over and out." In the silence of the dark his voice seemed to boom across the night. Catching his breath Grey started to make his way back in the direction he thought he'd come. Stumbling over a grave he apologized to the occupant and struggled back to his feet only to find himself looking face to face at a young lady. She was fair and wearing a red coat with leopard print scarf. Bit daring Grey thought to himself especially this time of night. "You'd be safer at home Miss. all this fog around."

"Yes, you're quite right officer, I'll do just that. Good night." Her sweet voice echoed as she hurried away into the fog and disappeared out of sight.

Shrugging his eyebrows Grey walked carefully through the dark out of the graveyard and made his way back to his post by the high street. Giving a little yawn he dawdled down the lonely street, not a soul in sight. Checking his watch by the nearest lamp post for light it was time to turn in, at last he thought. Swinging round his pace quickened as he made his way home.

"So much for your running skills Grey mate!" Bostin and Andrews were laughing in the locker room the next morning. The gossip of the police station always spread like wild fire, nothing was ever kept quiet for long.

"Yeh, you're funny lads, real funny." Grey replied in a rather grumpy voice. "You should have seen 'em. Bouncing over walls like kangaroos they were."

He gesticulated with his hand a bouncing motion to emphasize his point.

"Skippy the bouncing criminal! Yeh whatever mate." Andrews laughed as he left the room. Bostin was still laughing as he left too. Grey sat down on the bench in the locker room fumbling with his hat in his hands. Never taken seriously he pondered to himself. Ten years in the job and still the joke of the station. All he needed was a break. A case where he'd be at the right place at the right time. Running his fingers through his hair he stood, time to get on patrol. Pacing through the station it felt like all eyes were on him, watching him, waiting for him to fail. Again. Breathing a deep sigh Grey put on his hard hat and left the building.

The street looked so different in the daylight. So many shadows appeared at night, making you think things are there when they're not. Thinking back to last night Grey felt himself flush slightly at the thought of losing his mark.

"Morning officer Grey." A lady's voice cooed from the opposite side of the street. Looking over Grey tipped his hat at the group of ladies gathered. Unsure of who spoke he generally tipped his hat to the group who giggled on cue. Continuing down the street he heard the ladies gossiping behind him with a tiny whistle aimed at his uniform. Now really blushing he quickened his pace to get away from their stare.

Venturing round the corner he found himself back at the Aura graveyard, named so for the reputation of an eerie aura surrounding the yard which had never as yet been explained. Glancing towards the church there was a flash of red. Taking another look Grey saw nothing. Approaching cautiously to the side of church there was a lady in a red coat, bending over a grave. Tucking himself round the corner of a shop he peered round, keeping a visual on the lady. She stood and turned as if looking for someone. It was her. The lady from last night Grey realized. What was it with her and the graveyard, in fact she was remarkably close to where he must have bumped into her last night. His mind in overload he quickly ducked out of sight as she looked his direction. Carefully he cautioned a look back round the corner to find she had gone. Casually walking around the side of the church Grey saw that the lady was in fact no longer there. He paused momentarily. That smell, he sniffed, it was back again, drugs or something. Time for a rest Grey decided and headed back to the station ready for a bit more mockery.

The staff canteen was quiet so Grey had been lucky today, at least for the minute. Munching on his cheese sandwich Andrews strolled in and made a beeline straight for Grey. "How's the legs Grey? Got 'em working yet?" He laughed.

Grey smirked through his mouthful of food as he rolled his eyes at Andrews. More officers began to pile through the doors of whom appealed more to Andrews as he departed rather quickly to join them. Grey was grateful for the peace and quiet and enjoyed eating the rest of his sandwich without being bothered. The new arrivals were very chatty as they sat on the table behind Grey. All talking about a case that had come to light.

"Robberies they said." One of the lads was saying. "Random ones, here and there but they 'ave a pattern at the same time."

"I 'erd there's a lass involved." Another said in his northern accent. A few noises of approval came from the group enjoying the involvement of a lady.

"Red coat or something?" Andrews piped up joining in with the banter. This got Grey's attention. A red coat. Could it be that lady who was in the graveyard? Ideas rolling in his head Grey grabbed his hat and rushed out of the room much to the alarm of his colleagues who eventually started to laugh at him.

"Excuse me sir." Grey said entering the Chief Inspector's office.

"What is it Grey?" Chief Inspector Sommins replied looking up from his desk.

"It's this new case sir. About the red coat lady."

"Ah, yes. The case that the whole force wants to be involved with. What about it Grey?" Sommins huffed and sat back in his chair.

"It's just, well. I think I might know where she hides out, sir." Grey finished, remembering who he was talking to.

"Oh do you now? Where's that then Grey?" Sommins rose his eyebrows waiting an answer he was sure was going to disappoint him.

"Aura, sir." Grey said with a little nod.

"Aura you say? Why there in particular?" Sommins enquired pulling a cigar out of it's case.

"She was there last night during my chase and again today in my patrol she was back in the same place. Nearly exactly where I saw her last night." Grey looked pleased with himself after his little report.

"You get me proof Grey and then I'll believe you." He stood and held the door insinuating Grey to leave.

"Sir." Grey responded as he left the office. The door closed firmly behind him and Grey knew he was on his own. This was his chance to show them, all of them. Leaving the station Grey headed to Aura finding a shady spot to conceal himself ready for the lady to return. A few hours went by and it very quickly got dark. Grey switched his radio onto mute but still traceable in case of emergency. A twig snapped to his right hand side as his head whipped to the side to see what was there. Keeping very still Grey saw a blur of red emerge into his eye line. Feeling himself subconsciously tuck in deeper into his hiding place he watched as she crossed to the same bit of wall by the church. Looking round she didn't see him. From underneath her coat she pulled a small dark bag with a drawstring. Moving over to an insignificant looking grave she bent down still looking round. She had her back towards Grey so he couldn't tell what she was doing. She was about to move off when suddenly, that smell. His nose twitched, it was much stronger this close to the action. The lady was on the move, constantly looking around her. Waiting for her to move out of sight Grey quietly crept out of his hiding place and sped across the grass to the grave. It stank. The overpowering smell of cannabis was going right up his nose so he had to be quick. Running his hands along the grave he found a small opening in the ground. Putting his hand in it opened like a trapdoor, underneath was the small bag. Taking it out and replacing the lid Grey quickly ran as far as he could towards the station. All this running he thought to himself.

Jumping into the station Grey made for Sommins' office. With disbelief he discovered no one was there in the office. Grey opted to try the Superintendent. Marching round to the office Grey was relieved to find he was in. Gently knocking on the door Grey was asked to enter. On entry Grey greeted the Super and begged forgiveness for going over his

Inspector's head. Explaining the situation the Super accepted the apology and took the bag from Grey.

"You know Grey'" he spoke calmly. "I think that not only have you cracked the case of all these robberies we've been having recently." The Super began. "I also believe you may have found our leak in the department. You see the red coat, as she's referred to was more of an accomplice than the brain of the operation. I have had a couple of lads secretly investigating various members of the team and Sommins seemed the most likely."

"The man I was chasing through the graveyard? That was Sommins?" Grey uttered in astonishment. It certainly explained why his mark was so agile and fast, he knew what he was doing.

"I believe so, yes. This is just the proof I needed to prove his guilt." The Super smiled at Grey. Not a smile of sarcasm but a good smile.

"If I may ask sir. What was in the bag?" Grey was more intrigued than ever. He had never liked his boss but now he had a more concrete reason to do so.

"This bag. Has a certain something that belongs to a member of this station," he held up a police badge. "The remnants of used cannabis and," the Super paused putting his hand back into the bag. "A collection of rather lovely jewels that were reported stolen this evening." Pulling them out of the bag Grey saw the pearls which were absolutely stunning.

"The cannabis, was a signal that the goods were present." Grey hindered a guess. The Super nodded. Grey continued. "The smell also put anyone nearby off from going closer because of the stink, so they didn't find the stolen goods. But the police badge, I don't understand that?"

"A mere slip up. During a chase the night before a police badge was lost and was searched for by a certain lady in a red coat the following morning." The Super looked at Grey as the penny dropped.

"The badge was in the bag to be returned to Sommins, as it got dropped during the chase through the graveyard. She then went to find it and put in the bag for tonight's collection. So that was what she was doing." Realizing what the red coat lady was doing when he saw her in the afternoon.

The Super sat there grinning at Grey, picking up the receiver on his desk phone he simply said, " we've got him."


A couple of weeks later Grey stood admiring his new office door, his name reading across the front. Chief Inspector Grey. Smiling as he read it he opened his door and smoothed his hand along the desk. Sitting in his chair he rested his feet on the desk looking out at all his former colleagues dashing about in the corridor. Picking up the newspaper Grey read the main headline. 'Grey conquers Aura'. Lowering the paper back down he nodded to himself. "Yes he did." He smiled as he picked up the phone.

# 8. THE BLUE CURTAIN DROPS

Twenty years ago a beautiful, elegant looking theatre dominated the seafront. Passersby would stop to look up at the magnificent detail of the building taking in the hand carved scenes of cupid and other angels rejoicing across the top of the old building. Big blue double doors opened out into a spacious lobby decorated in royal blue and gold, with two desks on either side; one for reservations and tickets, the other for coats. Only the very best performed at the theatre. Flocks of people would come from around the country to say that had been to the 'Royal Theatre'. So aptly named as it's visitors frequently included nobility and household names. One autumn it all changed as disaster struck. Many theories surrounded what happened that day. Some say conspiracy to allow competitors a chance to flourish, others say an accident in the kitchens. Others say, murder.

"Here on your right hand side ladies and gentleman is the very sad sight of the old Royal Theatre." Gasps sounded through the tour bus as it came to a halt outside the derelict abandoned building. "Unfortunately" the conductor continued, "due to the building being unsafe we are unable to go inside." Silent sighs of disappointment echoed from many passengers though one or two of them wanted to know more.

"Excuse me sir?" A large American man piped up. "Can you tell us what happened to the place?"

The conductor raised an eyebrow as he took a large breath. The Royal always attracted attention on every tour bus. Being there that day never left him and never got any less painful when he told it's tale. Lowering his eyebrow to it's usual place the conductor began his well scripted and edited version of what happened that day.

"The Royal Theatre, shortened to the Royal, was destroyed twenty years ago by an explosion that erupted from beneath the auditorium. During this time the Royal was at the prime of it's life, the most popular theatre on the seafront both from show audiences and lovers of architecture. The theatre was about to celebrate forty years of being open but very sadly that was never to happen. Fortunately, in a way, when the disaster occurred there was no show on at that moment. The theatre was closed awaiting arrival of the next production team to construct their set for the next booking.

However in the incident seven people died and twelve more injured. Those twelve people survived to tell the tale. Until this day no one can be certain of what happened to cause such destruction, the theatre has been left to rest in peace as it were."

The out of the blue the conductor was asked a question he had never been asked before.

"And er," the American started, "were you one of that twelve?" Tilting his head back the man seemed to stare, waiting for an answer. The conductor was silent, his mind reeling. Thoughts and memories came flooding back to him as he momentarily gazed over at the theatre, flashbacks of sightings flew before his eyes.

"Yes. Yes I was." The conductor finally said quietly. A couple of camera flashes went off as some tourists took pictures of a newly found survivor of the historic Royal explosion. Blinking back a couple of tears he gave the order for the bus to continue on it's journey. The haunting visions of that day didn't leave him for the rest of the day, leaving him an unusually quiet tour guide. Arriving back at the depot the tourists disembarked from the bus thanking the driver for the safe journey. One of the last to climb down from the upper deck was the American who quizzed him about the theatre.

"Hey, look. Sorry I ask so many questions. This theatre has me very interested." He said. Turned out his name was Wallace as he shook hands with the conductor.

"Henry. Henry Baxter." The conductor shook Wallace's hand back. "So, what has you interested in the Royal?"

"Well. Seems to me like a great investment. I love old things and making them new again. The Royal could be an amazing addition to my portfolio." Handing over his business card Henry could see that Wallace was a well off business man he specialised in restorations. "I came over here to investigate this beauty. And I seem to have stumbled across someone who can help me out." Hinting subtly at Henry for being the helpful part.

"I don't see how I can help you Mr Wallace. I have no dealings with restoration projects." Henry admitted.

"No need for the Mr, Henry. Just Wallace to my friends." He grinned his big cheesy smile. "You can be very helpful. I' d like to know the ins and outs of what the Royal was in her prime. I can pay you more than this place. A lot more." Wallace added quietly. In most cases the use of money normally got Wallace exactly what he wanted. Even though he was a kind man he certainly knew how to use his assets to his advantage.

Henry was definitely interested in more money. His job did pay near enough peanuts for the amount of work he did. Deliberating the pros and cons of the proposition he realised he wanted to talk about the Royal. He had loved it so much and was devastated about it's abrupt end. The chance of bringing her back to life was a secret plea to relive times gone by.

"So, what do you say?" Wallace held out his hand for Henry to shake, to seal the deal. After a moment's looking at the hand in front of him Henry firmly shook it with a slight smile on his face. With a highly exaggerated hug from Wallace, Henry was taken back to the theatre where some men in hard hats were waiting. " Are you ready to visit old ghosts?" Wallace asked slipping on a hat and passing one over.

Taking the hat Henry stared at it. For the first time since it's destruction he was about to enter the Royal. He felt cold all of a sudden, as if seven ghosts were stood next to him. The hairs stood up on his neck as the charred blue doors were opened. Taking a couple of steps forward his lower lip trembled, a tear ran down his cheek as he saw the extent of the destruction inside the once beautiful lobby.

"Wow." Wallace exclaimed rather loudly. "What a waste." The men in hard hats led Henry and Wallace down a passage towards the auditorium. On reaching it there was a few moments silence. Lowering their heads they briefly remembered those who died that awful day. "Gentleman are we safe enough to take a small look downstairs?" Wallace asked the hard hats. Muttering reasons that they should not be there for long and other things they were granted a very quick visit to the under floor.

Traipsing down old familiar corridors old memories started to haunt Henry as he got closer to where the explosion had actually happened. Turning the corner into the kitchen Wallace briefly removed his hat in respect for what happened in that room. "God bless their souls." He simply said and put his hat back on. All the group nodded in agreement though not removing their hats as it wasn't really safe enough to do so. Heading back upstairs from orders of the hard hats they reconvened in the auditorium. "I want to do it." Wallace exclaimed abruptly. "I want the Royal to be just as she was. The elegant sophisticated queen of the seafront and 'the' theatre to visit. Gentleman, can it be done?"

Wallace and the hard hats formed a small group a little distance away from Henry, leaving him alone with his thoughts. All seven of those who had died were his friends. Every night after ushering people to their seats he'd go down to the kitchens to get some tea. They always had a laugh around the staff table. He remembered one particular night when the management had paid a surprise visit to the kitchens much to the alarm of the staff. Thinking they had done something wrong it appeared that they were being thanked for making the current show the most popular one that had ever been at the theatre. So to celebrate the management had brought down bottles of the finest champagne for the staff to enjoy at the close of the night. Smiling at the memory of that evening, the taste of the bubbly was luxurious, something none of them had ever tasted before.

"Henry?" All of a sudden he was back in the charred remains of the Royal. Looking over he saw Wallace beckoning him to go over to the group. "It's gonna happen, and I want you to be the manager of the project." Henry couldn't believe what was happening. "Only you can virtually see how she was back in her day. You can reconstruct her beauty and style, with a couple of changes." With that he hand gestured the effect of small changes. "I'll organise all the builders and supplies etcetera," another hand gesture emphasising his speech. "I want you to manage and advise and then be the general manager when we reopen. What do you say?"

Henry was almost speechless. Not four hours ago he was just a tour guide on a rickety bus. Now here he was on a new adventure with a very old friend. "I'd love to." He almost whispered.

"Great!" Wallace shook both his hands in extreme excitement. Clapping his hands together he set off with his phone making lots of calls getting in all his contacts to make the project run straight away. Within a week builders and cleaners started to arrive. The first big job was to clear out all of the damaged fittings which was near enough everything. The hard hats and insured professionals headed to the lower floor to begin clearing whilst Henry and some local volunteers, complete with their own hardhats, began clearing the lobby and auditorium. Everyone wanted to get involved in restoring the Royal. She had meant so much to everyone in the local community and it's visitors. The damage was cleared away and restoration began. Under strict orders to preserve and recreate the former style the builders began in the lower level, making it safe then working their way up. Henry worked mainly unseen during the process speaking to Wallace's contacts and scheduling acts to come and perform when the theatre reopened. Every time he visited the Royal it looked even more magnificent. Work was coming along fast and brilliantly. Original designs were coming back into place where they had always been, even royal blue curtains had been located to hang where they once hung. Lots of interest was building outside, eager to see the remastered theatre. Hardly anything was changed from the original setting. The one difference was in a room off from the lobby which was shielded by a blue curtain. Henry had been told that was the one place he could not go, as it was a surprise.

The time finally came seven months later for the theatre to reopen. Excitement was high as the first show to perform was set on the stage. The same show that was to perform just after the tragedy, twenty years ago. She looked stunning. Once again people were stopping to look up at her glory. Inside the lobby Wallace stood with Henry admiring the beauty around them. "She's gorgeous. Exactly as she was in almost every detail." Henry said proudly. Pride showed on his face as he looked round hardly remembering the state it was in before.

"Now for the final reveal before we open the doors." Striding over to the blue curtain, Wallace looked over at Henry as he pulled the cord. The blue curtain fell. Henry found his hands shoot to his mouth as he gasped at the sight. In the room stood a beautiful mahogany bar with gold rails. A few tall tables with gold stools adorned with royal blue cushions were spread throughout the room. Behind the bar were lined different wine bottles, all different countries and vintages. However in the centre of the display was a column of the same bottle which was all too familiar. That famous champagne they had all drunk before the tragedy happened in the kitchens. Above it the bar was simply called 'The Seven Bar'. Tears welled in Henry's eyes. "For all seven of those who lost their lives in that fateful incident." Wallace said putting his hand on Henry's shoulder. Wiping the tears from his face Henry hugged Wallace before they stood by the big blue doors, and smiling at each other, opened them.

# 9. EVERGREEN COPSE PART 3

Sitting in Hazel's front room Ben took a sip of his glass of whisky, grimacing as it hit the back of his throat. He didn't usually drink whisky but he felt he needed a stiffer drink than normal.

"She was so lovely. Me and her at the little table together." Ben mumbled to anyone who was listening. The group had left the crime scene and were waiting for Hazel's return. "It was our second date you know." He continued. "One more and we would have been official." Sniffing back a threatening tear he took another sip of his drink, much to the same effect as his previous sip.

"You would have made a lovely couple." Nora remarked, trying to lighten the mood.

"I'm really sorry everyone, I really need to go home. Mother needs help to get ready for bed. She's probably wondering where I've got to." Hettie piped up. Time was getting on. Dusk had set in and understandably Hettie wanted to get home before it was completely dark. No one felt safe at the moment to travel home in the dark.

"I'll walk you home Hettie. Safety in numbers." Alfred rose from his seat on the sofa, slipping on his coat.

"Thank you Alfred that would be kind."Hettie smiled adding her hat to her coat and boots ensemble. "Goodnight everyone, give Hazel a hug for me." With that they departed into the fast approaching night.

"You can go home too if you like Ben. I'll stay for Hazel. She's going to need some company tonight." Nora said quietly, breaking the silence.

"No I'm good." He answered. "I'm where I need to be. Even if I can't be of any help at least I'm here to offer some support."

Sitting in silence they both sat and waited for Hazel to get home. Ben got up a few times to look out of the window to watch for Hazel only to resign back to the sofa. Neither of them wanted to leave in case Hazel returned while they were out looking for her. Minutes turned to hours and they both drifted off to sleep still waiting, still sat on the sofa.

Morning came and Nora woke first with a start, wondering at first where she was. Realizing she'd fallen asleep on Hazel's sofa she wondered up the stairs to check on her. Knocking on her bedroom door there was no answer. Opening the door slightly Nora peered through the crack only to see that Hazel had not been in there, the bed had not been slept in. Closing the door again Nora searched the whole house, still no sign of Hazel. Back in the front room Ben was stirring. With a groan he opened his eyes.

"How is she?" He asked in a slightly croaky voice. Blinking away the sleep in his eyes.

"She isn't here." Nora remarked concern stretched across her face.

"Not here!" Ben was suddenly wide awake. Jumping off the sofa he pulled on his brown jacket. "Where could she be? Maybe she went with the police last night." Pacing the sitting room Ben was desperately trying to think where to search first.

"I don't see why she would." Nora replied. Pulling her phone out of her pocket Nora dialed Hazel's and listened to it ring. "No answer." She concluded.

"Let's go look for her." Ben commanded. Nodding in agreement Nora grabbed her coat and went outside with Ben. Leaving the house they decided to head to the crime scene first, to see if anyone knew where Hazel went last night. On arrival there was no one there. The body had been taken away but the tape was still attached around the area telling them not to cross. Once again Nora tried to call Hazel's phone, listening to it ring in her hear, she heard something peculiar. Ben heard it too, he walked over to the tape and ducked under. Nora strode over to the tape but didn't cross watching Ben search the ground. He picked something up off the ground with his back to her. Turning round there was something black in his hand. Walking over to the tape Ben held up a phone, the one that Nora was ringing. Nora gasped. Hazel's phone, but where was Hazel?

"Looks like she was writing a message when she dropped it." Ben said looking at the screen. "She only wrote two words. Saved in drafts, looks like it was going to be for you." Ben handed Nora the phone so she could see. Accessing the draft message she read the two words.

"He's here." Nora looked confused momentarily, then her eyes flashed. A look of horror appeared on her face and suddenly she knew what might have happened to Hazel.

Ben looked at her quizzically. "Why that's a face." He smirked. "Two words that seem to set you on edge."

Nora looked at Ben. Her face paled and she felt very cold, frozen with fear. She knew. She knew who he was. "Erm Ben. I need to go home, get a change of clothes." She stammered as she slowly began to inch her legs back in the direction they had just come from.

"Are you feeling alright Nora?" He asked, a shadow was passing across his face.

"Yes. Yes. Fine." Nora turned and felt her legs struggling to walk. She had to get away. Her legs were stiff as wood. Her mouth was trembling, she wanted to scream but she couldn't, knowing that if she did she'd regret it. Her legs started to feel a little movement making it easier to walk, she picked up her pace slightly.

Ben watched her walk away. The shadow over him darkened as his normally friendly gaze turned hard and cold. Glaring at her he flared his nostrils. Stalking after Nora his large paces quickly caught up with Nora's stiffly moving speed. He knew. Turning a corner Nora quickly whipped out her phone and dialed 999, asked for the police then dropped it back in pocket whilst still connected. Her legs were just starting to move more freely, ready to bolt when a pair of hands clamped down on her shoulders. She shrieked.

"Oh. No. You. Don't." The dark voice behind her whispered into her ear. Pulling her back the figure swung Nora round and before she screamed they covered her mouth and dragged her away.

The room she was in was dark and chilly, yet strangely familiar. A small candle was in the corner, Nora recognized it now. Her basement at home.

Nora looked up, her eyes widened. She couldn't scream, she was tied and gagged. In the corner was Hazel. She was sat there spinning a dagger round in her fingers. Noticing that she was being watched she through the dagger to the ground and laughed.

"So you found me." She cackled. "Last place to look, never is the obvious place to look." Hazel continued, speaking as if possessed, staring in to space as she spoke. "You know. The best part is you didn't have a clue. All them years ago you didn't know, and you still don't." Crouching on the floor and grabbing Nora's chin firmly Hazel spoke into her face. "It was me." Throwing away Nora's face Hazel began to laugh uncontrollably. "Giving evidence was the worst thing you could have done. All this time you thought he was a man. Ha. So stupid Nora. Hasn't anyone told you? Running away makes the chase more fun." Slapping Nora hard across the face Hazel resumed her seat in the corner. Nora whimpered in pain, her cheek feeling red hot and pulsing with pain. Tears began to fall.

"Such a shame. The police never did find the one who strangled the housekeeper. They were sure that it was the mystery man who broke into your father's office and strangled him. Same style means same person apparently. Getting into your father's office was easy. He liked long legs and short skirts." She grinned wryly at Nora who fiercely tried to kick out of her ropes. "I knew what I wanted, I just needed him out of the way. Only what

69

do I find? The blueprints gone, and his little princess running off from the bottom of the drainpipe with a mysterious backpack." Rising up again Hazel retrieved her dagger that was on the floor, Nora gulped a little too loudly. Staring at her Hazel sniggered. "Like it do you? Sorry to disappoint but it's not for you." Nora breathed a little relief. "I have something much better for you." Reaching behind a wooden box Hazel pulled out a long piece of blue rope. Nora instantly recognized it as being the same kind that was left around her father's neck when he was murdered. "Same I used on Rachel, so it's second hand I'm afraid."

Advancing towards her victim Nora tried to scream but she was still gagged. Suddenly a loud bang sounded and the room filled with light. "Freeze!" A loud voice yelled down into the basement.

"How are you feeling?" Ben asked looking down at Nora kindly.

"Bit shaky still." She answered trying to hold on to her mug of tea without spilling it.

"Ben's a hero." Alfred chirped from his perch on the mantelpiece. "He followed you as far as he could without being seen by your attacker. Then he came and got me to phone the police."

"Only to find that someone else had already thought of it." Ben added, glancing at Nora.

"My phone?" Nora remembered dialing for the police before she was dragged away.

"Tracked your phone didn't they. Got the whole thing recorded." Alfred smiled smugly.

"But why Rachel?" Nora asked quietly.

"Somehow she worked it out. We'll never know how she did but she must have called Hazel even though she told us Rachel did no such thing. Then alerting Hazel that Rachel needed removing before she could get to you. To warn you." Alfred explained.

"What were the blueprints for?" Ben asked sitting next to Nora.

"An oil refinery. It was secret you see. The location anyway. If she got hold of that she could have gained a fortune." Nora looked up from her tea and smiled. "Father knew there was people after the prints as there was a leak in the department. So I secretly took them which is why she must have seen me running from the building."

"She didn't get the prints then?" Alfred asked putting down his empty mug on the coffee table.

"No. No she didn't."

"But where are they? I mean you must have put them in a really safe place?"

Ben enquired, feeling very curious.

"Like Hazel said to me. The last place you look, never is the obvious place to look." Nora felt a bit brighter all of a sudden, pride washed over her as she finally clicked that she'd pulled a fast one on Hazel all those years ago.

"Nora." Alfred said. "Where did you hide the prints?" Suspense filled the room as Nora grinned broadly.

"In my Father's pocket in his coffin." She began to laugh and the boys laughed with her.

# 10. THE MIRRORS

The young girl sat in her room all alone and stared at the clock on the wall. Five o' clock in the afternoon. Dinner would soon be ready at the call of her mother from the bottom of the stairs. Her homework sat on the desk which was attached underneath her bed, a little red lamp was switched on at the side. Science was finished and English half way there. She just sat there staring into space, not thinking anything. Coming out of her trance she turned back to the homework in front of her. A good girl at school always did homework the day she received it, whether it took five minutes or five hours she made sure she got it done. Writing away the far away call from her mother declared that dinner was on the table. Putting the lid back on her pen she switched off the red lamp and descended to the kitchen for dinner. Her brother and father were already at the table whilst mother plated up the dinner to put on the table.

Sitting in her chair she sat quietly whilst her brother and father argued amongst themselves, a constant conflict of who knew more of whatever subject they were talking about. No matter what the subject was the argument was still the same. Mother put the plates on the table which everyone thanked her for. Straight after dinner was consumed the boys restarted their battle over a new subject, their main problem was that they were so similar they clashed on a regular basis. Mother and the girl rolled their eyes at the never ending war and carried out the washing up. All put away the girl retreated back to her room to continue her homework.

A little knock on the door. "Can I come in?" Mother said from the other side of the door.

"Of course mother." The girl answered. Opening the door mother crept in gently holding a cup of hot tea. Coming over to the desk she put the tea in a place it wouldn't get spilt. "Thank you."

"It's getting late Lucy. Have you still got a lot more to do?" Asked mother looking down at all the books on the desk.

"I'm nearly there." Lucy huffed flicking through all the pages she'd already written.

"Just make sure you get to bed soon okay." Mother said stroking Lucy's hair and kissing her forehead.

"Yes mother." Lucy answered smiling up at her. "Goodnight." She added.

"Goodnight Lucy." Closing the door, mother crossed the landing to her bedroom.

Left alone to finish her homework Lucy's mind went back to the matter in hand. About an hour later she finally finished her work and closed up the books. Despite all the hours she put into her homework she never got the best grades, but English was the one subject she liked doing so she didn't mind too much. Climbing the ladder to her bed she got snuggled in as she used her umbrella to switch the light off, in order to save her from getting back out to switch it off. Laying in the darkness the conveyor belt of thoughts started. What was she going to do at school tomorrow, was her homework good enough, when would she find a man. Anything and everything filtered through her mind as she drifted off to sleep.

Walking to school in the morning the air was fresh with a chill. Her big coat kept her warm and the colour of orange mad sure she was seen by all traffic. She liked orange but blue was starting to become her favorite colour. Walking through the gates the sense of dread hit her once again. Lucy really didn't like going to school, she never told her parents what happened there, she just kept it all to herself.

First class of the day was German. She liked languages and was reasonably good at them. Putting her bag on a seat third row from the front she sat in the corner and waited for it to start. The rest of the class were filtering through the door in their huddles of friends. A group of boys walked in as if they owned the place, making lots of noise and causing a general nuisance. Swarming towards Lucy's side of the classroom one of the boys walked right in front of her, grabbed her bag off of the desk and threw it across the classroom on to the front desk on the other side of the classroom. The other boys laughed at her. "We're sitting here." The cocky boy said to her. Another started kicking the back of her chair to force her to move. Standing up Lucy took her coat and moved over to where the boy had thrown her bag and sat in the corner by the window and directly joined onto the teachers desk. The teacher then came in the room and the class settled down though the boys were still snickering at Lucy. She felt herself go red, looking down at her exercise book she felt a tear well up in her eye. Blinking it away quickly she clenched her lip with her teeth to stop herself. Lowering her bag onto the floor Lucy subtly peered inside to make sure nothing was broken by pretending to look for something inside. The rest of the lesson went quickly and the five minute changeover happened to move rooms to the next lesson.

Maths bored Lucy, she was not very good at it and didn't like it but she did have a nice teacher. Sat at the front on her own by the window Lucy done her best with the work set but didn't ask for any help as she didn't have the courage to raise her hand.

Lunchtime came and Lucy found a corner in the school field to sit in. Eating her ham sandwich mother had made her she sat quietly minding her own business dwelling on the events of the morning. Finishing her sandwich she dug out her packet of crisps and her school planner. Last lesson of the day was science. Lucy wasn't very good at science either. She really tried but she could never get her head around formulas or equations. Waiting outside the science lab the class mucked around in the corridor showing off to their friends. The teacher arrived and unlocked the room. Everyone dashed in to get their seats, no one wanting to sit on the front bench. No more space in the room Lucy had to sit at the front, no stool. Looking round the room Lucy grabbed a vacant stool from the back of the room and brought it to the front to sit on. Two other girls who were late had to sit on the front bench too but as far away as they possibly could from Lucy. The teacher announced they were going to do an experiment using Bunsen burners, so the class were to pair up or make a three. Lucy looked over to the girls on her bench and smiled. They both glared at her in return, looking her up and down making Lucy feel the size of an ant.

The class got on with the experiment in their pairs with all the equipment and the teacher helping them all out. Lucy sat on her own on the front bench. It was as though she wasn't even there. Not one person spoke to her or acknowledged her. She just sat there as the class around her buzzed around playing with the equipment. Looking down her hair fell about her face as a few tears ran down her face onto the bench. Nobody noticed, nobody cared. Homework was set based on the experiment from the lesson and class was dismissed. Pulling on her coat and taking her bag Lucy quickly made her way out of the room and out of the school grounds as quick as she could. Walking out of the school gates her pace slowed as she made her way home through the town.

Walking in the door Lucy called to say it was her. "I'm home."

"Hello Lucy," mother said as she went through into the kitchen. "How was your day?" She asked.

"It was alright thank you mother." Lucy feebly smiled. "Lots of homework again. I did German today, I can tell you how old I am and when my birthday is in German." Lucy said her smile spreading a little.

"Very impressive. I used to do Spanish when I was at school. I used to really enjoy it, can't remember much of it now though. Father is working nights today so he won't be with us for dinner today and your brother is out at dancing class so shall we watch something together after dinner?"

"Yes I'd like that." Lucy beamed. Lucy loved her mother. She was her best and only friend. She'd tell her mother nearly anything. Climbing the stairs to her room the arduous task of homework started again. German homework was easy so it didn't take long. Maths she did during lunch while sat on the field, just science left. Since it was based on the experiment it was very hard as Lucy didn't get to do it. Reading the textbook she tried to figure out the answer for herself. A couple of hours later she descended to join mother who was just finishing cooking the dinner. Lucy helped the last little bit and they ate together and talked for what seemed hours.

"It's so nice and quiet without the rentagobs." Mother laughed as they washed up the plates. Moving into the sitting room the girls put on a murder mystery to watch on the television. It finished and it was time for bed. Once again climbing the ladder Lucy got into bed and switched off the light in her unique fashion. Laying down she thought about the day. Her eyes welled up as she thought about her bag being thrown across the room, being laughed at and being invisible. She let the tears fly as there was no one to watch her. Holding on to one of her teddies she sobbed herself to sleep.

A few years later Lucy was in sixth form at that same school. The years had passed with everyday being the same. Lucy believed it might of been different as she was older but nothing changed. Her mother was still her only friend alongside all her animals in her bedroom. A task was set to organize a week of work experience and all the class was asked what they wanted to do. When it came to Lucy she was honest in her answer.

"I want to dance on stage." She said in front of all the class. They looked at her and laughed, they didn't stop laughing for some time. The teacher was kind and tried to quieten the class which eventually worked. Lucy wrote to many places asking if they took placements for a week. With a stroke of luck one place said yes. So during the summer Lucy, her parents and her brother went to the holiday park where Lucy joined in with the entertainments crew for a week. She loved it. Being somewhere where not one person knew of her terrible time at school and couldn't make fun of her. In effect she made one friend of whom she stayed in touch with for a good many years later. 'Lovely' he called her. She smiled whenever she was with him, never having felt what it was like to have a friend. Lucy made some impact that she was asked to rejoin them as part of the real crew the following year.

Unbelievably happy Lucy joined the entertainments troop much to the disbelief of most of the year of students at school, not to mention the teachers. The first couple of months went by really fast Lucy loved her independence and being with her friend who happened to still be there. However old times began to haunt Lucy as familiar things began to happen. Out of eighteen people being in the team there was only one person who was not involved in any show of any sort, Lucy. Feeling rather left out Lucy carried on as normal just thinking because she was new she'd get the chance another time. During the time at the park she had got very close to the friend she made during the previous encounter for her work experience. However this had not gone unnoticed by her friend's partner. Perhaps feeling threatened by Lucy she asked what it was that Lucy could do.

"I sing and Megan here is a trained dancer, but what can you do?" Asking over the microphone in front of a room full of guests, Lucy was powerless, the feeling from her schooldays she knew so well had returned. "Nothing," the partner continued. "You're just a waste of space really aren't you?" Feeling highly embarrassed and humiliated Lucy did nothing. A room full of people looking at her in silence.

The end of season came and Lucy did not return to the park the following year. In the time of her life when she should have been looking at clothes and pouting in mirrors she hid from them and covered up the mirrors so she couldn't see what she looked like, she didn't want to see.

A couple of years later Lucy managed to pluck up some courage to audition for a different company of holiday parks and within a week was offered a job. "I'm in!" Lucy cried when she got her letter in the post. Her parents told her how pleased they were for her but secretly they worried it was going to be a repeat of her experience at the other park. However it was to be very different indeed. Her small group of colleagues at the new park welcomed her with open arms. Instead of mocking her quietness they used it as a nickname. A few months down the line Lucy met Lawrence who transferred to her park. Within a month Lawrence had asked Lucy to go out with him. For the first time in her life she felt wanted. She told him all about her experiences and what she did in her spare time. He listened.

"What do you see when you look in the mirror?" He asked.

"I don't. I never look in the mirrors, they remind me of what I am." Lucy said sadly. "A loner. A boring individual. And ugly." Sniffing back a tear Lucy wiped her eyes.

"I'll tell you what I see." Lawrence replied. He reached up to the mirror and removed the sheet covering it. "I see a wonderful little lady who is polite, beautiful and extremely kind and caring. You know what else I see?" He asked as he put his arms round Lucy, looking in the mirror. "I see us." He smiled at her in the mirror making her smile back at him. "Can I keep you?" He whispered in her ear.

Spinning round Lucy put her arms round him. "Yes." She answered as she hugged him and held him for the rest of her life.

# AUTHOR'S AFTERWORD

A Collection Of Shorts is a very special book to me. A lot of people have influenced the characters along with their personalities, most of them reflecting real people in real life stories that have actually happened. Some tales are direct from my own personal experiences in life, some not as cheerful as others but there's always a happy ending. Other tales are derived from everyday speculations that act as a muse to create plots for the characters I see every day. Having a mixture of stories provides a canvas which can be used to extend or create more tales using these fictional plots and characters. Here is my own little slot to say thank you for reading these stories and I hope you've enjoyed them as much as I enjoyed writing them.

# ABOUT THE AUTHOR

Katie A Nimmo was born in England, September 1986. Born and bred in the Surrey countryside Katie had a quiet upbringing around the virtues of family and working hard to make dreams become reality. These ethics have led to many of her aspirations coming true. Previous to her writing career Katie performed on the stage for several years contrary to the popular belief of her shyness among those in her school hood years. Katie's newfound confidence to defeat the odds led her to pursue her dream of writing which has led to many adventures both on and off the page.